Problem Solving Safari
ART

Searching for opportunities to teach
problem solving skills during art experiences

By Barbara F. Backer, M.Ed.
Illustrated by Gary Mohrman

Totline® Publications
A Division of Frank Schaffer Publications, Inc.
Torrance, California

This book is dedicated with love to the daughters my sons brought me, Karen and Jennifer. Thank you for mastering the art of keeping my sons happy.

—B.F.B.

Managing Editor: Kathleen Cubley
Editor: Elizabeth McKinnon
Contributing Editors: Gayle Bittinger, Carol Gnojewski, Susan Hodges, Jean Warren
Copyeditor: Kris Fulsaas
Proofreader: Miriam Bulmer
Editorial Assistant: Durby Peterson
Graphic Designer: Sarah Ness
Graphic Designer (Cover): Brenda Mann Harrison
Production Manager: Melody Olney

©1997 by Totline® Publications. All rights reserved. Except for reproducing the Parent Flyer page for noncommercial use or including brief quotations in a review, no part of this book may be reproduced or utilized in any form or by any means, electronic or mechanical, including photocopying, recording, or by any information storage and retrieval system, without written permission from the publisher.

ISBN: 1-57029-118-7

Printed in the United States of America
Published by Totline® Publications.
Editorial Office: P.O. Box 2250
　　　　　　　　　Everett, WA 98203
Business Office: 23740 Hawthorne Blvd.
　　　　　　　　　Torrance, CA 90505

20 19 18 17 16 15 14 13 12 11 10 9 8 7 6 5 4 3 2

INTRODUCTION

Learning to solve problems is probably one of the most important skills we can teach young children. However, problem solving cannot be taught as a subject unto itself.

To learn problem solving techniques, children must be given the opportunity to identify meaningful problems and encouraged to try solving them whenever and wherever they occur.

It is not difficult to find problem solving opportunities—they are happening all day long. The purpose of this book is to help teachers become more aware of these opportunities when they are in the art area with their children.

In *Problem Solving Safari—Art*, 20 scenarios are presented, each centering around a particular problem. These meaningful problems, with their possible solutions, come from children's real play and point of view. The problems provide springboards for children to become creative and discover how or why things work. Various problem solving steps are suggested to help your children identify problems and then brainstorm to seek workable solutions, and your role in encouraging this process is outlined. There are no right or wrong solutions—all the children's ideas are respected. If they try to solve a problem and it does not work, this too becomes a valuable learning experience. It allows them to analyze and evaluate a solution, then try again.

To help stretch your children's thinking skills, a list of children's books with art-centered problem solving situations is provided. Also, a reproducible Parent Flyer is included to use as an invitation for parents to become a part of the learning process and join their children in art experiences as problem solvers.

Problem Solving Safari—Art, describes many open-ended opportunities for arousing your children's curiosity, encouraging their creativity, promoting their critical thinking and social interactions, and strengthening their physical abilities. All of these opportunities provide an important beginning for the development of your children's problem solving skills.

CONTENTS

Steps for Problem Solving 6

Your Role 7

Unexpected Rubbings 8

Holes in the Paper 9

Mashed-In Marker Tips 10

Smeared Art Pastels 11

Paper Strips Galore 12

A Stained Wall 13

What a Mess! 14

A Big, Big Box 15

She's Coloring on My Paper! 16

That's Ugly 17

He's Not Sharing! 18

Colored Tissue Marks 19

Stopped-Up Glue Bottles 20

Drippy Paint 21

No Paintbrushes 22

Why Doesn't This Stuff Stick? 23

Mixing Colors 24

How Do You Make Handprints? 25

The Modeling Dough Is Icky 26

Dried-Out Markers 27

Parent Flyer 28

Children's Book List 29

STEPS FOR PROBLEM SOLVING

Below are steps that you can take with your children when determining problems, developing solutions, and putting those solutions into action.

1. **IDENTIFY** – Determine and discuss the problem. It should be meaningful, interesting, and appropriate for young children.

2. **BRAINSTORM** – Encourage your children to think about possible solutions. Listen to and respect all of their ideas. Keep a record of the solutions suggested in case the children want to try more than one.

3. **SELECT** – Help your children examine the advantages and disadvantages of various solutions and then choose one that seems workable.

4. **EXPLORE AND IMPLEMENT** – Let your children gather the necessary materials and resources and then try out the solution they decided upon.

5. **EVALUATE** – With your children, observe and discuss whether the solution to the problem was successful. If appropriate, help the children think of changes they might want to make in the idea they tried. Or, encourage them to try other solutions.

YOUR ROLE

Your role in facilitating the development of your children's problem solving behaviors is that of encourager and guide. Be sure to allow plenty of time and space for the children to brainstorm and try out their ideas. Below are other ways you can help.

* Observe carefully to see how you can facilitate the problem solving process. For instance, provide or add special materials when needed. Also, encourage your children to observe in order to verify what is happening.

* Turn any mistake into a learning experience. Help your children analyze why a solution did not work out.

* Promote discussion, interaction, and collaboration. As your children work together, help them to be patient and persistent in their explorations.

* Throughout the day, model problem solving skills in natural ways. However, avoid solving your children's problems for them. Trust them to come up with solutions!

* Listen to, acknowledge, and support your children's ideas. Respect their suggestions and encourage them to value one another's viewpoints.

* Provide easy access to stimulating materials. If your children need assistance, help them learn how to use the materials in diverse ways.

* Arouse curiosity. Ask open-ended questions that begin with "What if?" or "Why do you suppose?" to foster creative—and critical—thinking.

* Encourage experimentation. Let your children know that it is all right to take a guess or try a new idea (always keeping in mind the children's safety). Help them understand that there are no "perfect" solutions.

UNEXPECTED RUBBINGS

A boy is coloring at the art table. As he works, an outline, or rubbing, of a shape appears on his paper. Your children want to know how this has happened so that they can make rubbings too. What can they do?

Children's Possible Solutions

1. The boy decides to color all over his paper to see if more shapes appear.

2. A girl suggests that the boy try coloring with different crayons.

3. Other children say, "Look under your paper." When the boy does so, he discovers a paper shape that matches the rubbing. Your children find other paper shapes in the scrap box and decide to use them to try making their own rubbings.

Your Role

Provide crayons in a variety of colors. Encourage the boy to continue exploring.

Encourage the child's actions. Ask him to describe what is happening.

Make sure that the scrap box contains a variety of paper shapes as well as shapes cut from different-textured paper.

Extending the Experience

- Make rubbings of a variety of items, such as coins, ribbons, doilies, or textured placemats.

- Outdoors, make rubbings of items such as tree bark, leaves, cement walkways, trike pedals, or swing chains.

- Make rubbings of the bottoms of the children's athletic shoes.

Skills Used
Motor Skills
Critical Thinking Skills

8 ♦ Problem Solving Safari—Art

HOLES IN THE PAPER

Several children are reclining on the carpet, drawing pictures on paper. Their pencils are pushing through the paper and making holes. How can the children continue with their artwork?

Children's Possible Solutions

1. One child decides to repair the holes in his paper with tape.

2. Another child wants to put a book or a magazine under her paper to provide a firm surface.

3. Other children decide to incorporate the holes in their papers into their artwork. The children try using other items, such as crayons and chalk, to see if they will make holes too.

Your Role

Have tape available for your children's use. Help them discover that placing tape on the back of their papers hides the repairs and keeps the tape from covering their pictures.

Support this suggestion by having magazines and other hard, portable surfaces available. The covers of discarded wallpaper sample books work well.

Support your children's efforts and have safe items available. Ask, "Which items make the biggest holes? The smallest? Which work best? Why?"

Extending the Experience

- Look around for different kinds of holes. Some examples are holes in lace-up shoes, window screens, fences, suitcase handles, hoops, and rings.

- Make sieves by punching holes in various materials, such as pieces of aluminum foil, sheets of waxed paper, or cardboard shoeboxes. Which materials are easiest to punch holes in? Which work best as sieves?

- In the sides of large cardboard cartons, cut holes for your children to crawl through.

Skills Used
Motor Skills
Critical Thinking Skills
Creative Thinking Skills

Problem Solving Safari—Art

MASHED-IN MARKER TIPS

Your children take out felt tip markers to use for their artwork. But when they try to draw, they discover that the markers won't work because the tips are all mashed in. What can the children do?

Children's Possible Solutions

1. In an attempt to pull out the marker tips, several children dig at them with their fingers.

2. Other children suggest trying to dig out the tips with scissors.

3. One child says, "We need new markers."

Your Role

Encourage your children's efforts and praise their persistence.

Acknowledge the children's solution. Then discuss scissor safety and how scissors should properly be used.

Facilitate discussion about how the markers might have become damaged. How will the children protect new markers?

Extending the Experience

- Use mashed-in markers to make indentations when playing with modeling dough.

- Mash golf tees into modeling dough that has been placed in a large margarine tub.

- Recite and act out fingerplays that include hammering motions.

Skills Used
Motor Skills
Critical Thinking Skills

SMEARED ART PASTELS

When your children use art pastels, the colors often smudge and rub off on their hands and clothes. How can they prevent this?

Children's Possible Solutions

Your Role

1. One child decides to paint a layer of glue over his creation to make the colors stay put.

Encourage the child's problem solving by providing brushes and glue. Help the child evaluate his method while the glue is wet and again when the glue is dry.

2. A girl decides to paint over her drawing with water to make colors that will not rub off.

Encourage the child by providing water and brushes. Help her evaluate her method while the paper is wet and again when it is dry.

3. A boy tries to wipe off the excess dust by rubbing his drawing with a wad of facial tissue. This creates a smeared abstract picture.

Encourage the boy's efforts. Ask him to describe what happened to his drawing and help him evaluate his method.

Extending the Experience

- Use sidewalk chalk to draw pictures outdoors. Observe over time to see if the colors remain sharp and bright.

- Dip art pastels in water, then use them to draw on dark-colored construction paper. Compare the results with drawings made with dry pastels.

- Use art pastels to draw on wet construction paper. Does the color smudge when the paper is wet? When the paper dries?

Skills Used
Motor Skills
Critical Thinking Skills

Problem Solving Safari—Art ♦ 11

PAPER STRIPS GALORE

Your children find a lot of paper strips left over from another art project. What can they do with the strips?

Children's Possible Solutions

Your Role

1. Several children suggest using the strips to make a paper chain.

Encourage the children's efforts. Offer to display the chain for everyone to admire.

2. Another child demonstrates how to make 3-D art by gluing the ends of several strips to a cardboard base and then twisting the strips before gluing down the other end. He weaves additional strips over and under the glued strips.

Help the child describe how he constructed his creation.

3. A girl demonstrates how to staple several strips together at angles to make a long zigzag. She uses this on the floor as a road for toy cars.

Compliment the child on her creative idea.

Extending the Experience

- Make a paper chain calendar. Count the links to see how many days until a special event, such as a field trip. Each day, remove a link of the chain. On the day of the big event, remove the final link.

- Using strips of colored paper, make pattern chains, such as yellow-green-yellow-green or red-red-blue-red-red-blue.

Skills Used
Motor Skills
Critical Thinking Skills

A STAINED WALL

A wall in your room has stains on it. Your children all agree that the stains are unsightly. What can they do?

Children's Possible Solutions

1. Several children think that they should try washing the stains off the wall.

2. Other children suggest making a large mural on paper to hang over the stain.

Your Role

Provide buckets of water and sponges along with towels for mopping up any spills.

Facilitate discussion about the size, color, and topic of the mural. Provide materials and encouragement. When the mural is completed and hung, invite parents and other classes to come see how different the wall looks.

Extending the Experience

- Use large house-painting brushes and buckets of water to "paint" the outside walls of your center.
- Make other murals. Use them to decorate inside doors, walls outside the room, and bulletin boards.

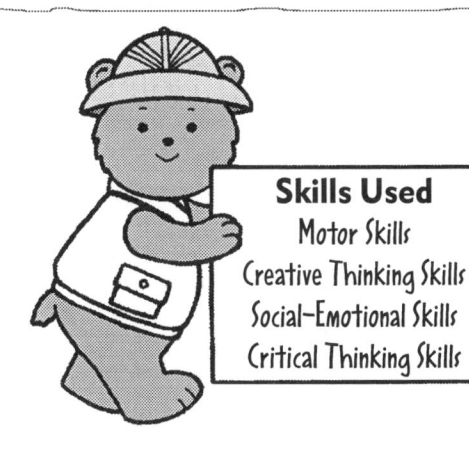

Skills Used
Motor Skills
Creative Thinking Skills
Social-Emotional Skills
Critical Thinking Skills

Problem Solving Safari—Art ◆ 13

WHAT A MESS!

The art table is extremely messy with marker streaks, wet and dried glue, small pieces of modeling dough, and other materials stuck to it. What can your children do?

Children's Possible Solutions

1. Several children try using sponges and brushes from the water table and hand soap from the bathroom to clean the art table.

2. One child suggests making a rule: "People who mess up must clean up!"

3. Other children suggest covering the art table with newspaper early each day. They think this will protect the table and make cleanup easier.

Your Role

Encourage your children's efforts. Afterward ask, "Did the cleaning materials work? What else might we try?" Provide safe materials, and caution the children to clean up spills.

Have your children discuss this idea. How will they enforce the rule? Provide any materials the children request to facilitate their idea, such as a sign-in sheet or a poster stating the rule.

Remind your children to bring in newspapers, and provide a place to store them. Help the children decide on a fair way to delegate the daily job of covering the table.

Extending the Experience

- Provide materials to encourage cleaning all parts of your room. Include items such as a small broom and a dustpan, a small mop, a feather duster, a non-scratch scouring pad, and nontoxic cleaners.

- Encourage outdoor cleanup too. Pick up trash in the play yard and sweep walkways.

Skills Used
Social-Emotional Skills
Motor Skills

14 ◆ Problem Solving Safari—Art

A BIG, BIG BOX

A parent has brought in a large appliance box for your children to play with. How can they use it?

Children's Possible Solutions

1. Your children suggest ways to use the box: as a fort outdoors; as a hiding place outdoors; as a quiet reading place indoors; as a small playhouse.

2. Several children suggest finding more boxes so that all of the desired items can be made.

3. Several other children want to use the original appliance box plus any additional cartons to make a long, long tunnel.

Your Role

Discuss all ideas. Ask, "Since there is only one box, how can we decide which idea to choose?"

Bring in more boxes of all sizes. (Furniture and appliance stores and office supply companies will donate large cartons.) Discuss with your children how they will use the boxes, and provide materials such as felt tip markers, tape, and glue.

Brainstorm ideas for accomplishing this idea. How can the children make the tunnel long? Offer assistance if they need help.

Extending the Experience

* Illustrate and send dictated thank-you notes to the people who provided boxes.

* Ask the children to bring in smaller boxes to use in the various centers in your room.

* Decorate a large carton to make a present for another class.

Skills Used
Social-Emotional Skills
Motor Skills
Creative Thinking Skills

Problem Solving Safari—Art ◆ 15

SHE'S COLORING ON MY PAPER!

While several of your children are coloring at the art table, a girl reaches over and begins to color on a boy's paper. The second child howls, and the other children at the table are upset. What can the children do?

Children's Possible Solutions | Your Role

1. The boy and some of the other children want the girl to be banished from the table.	Help the boy express his feelings and tell the girl why he is upset. Help all the children understand that "in this safe classroom, we try not to do things that hurt others' feelings."
2. Several other children suggest that the boy color on the girl's paper to "show her how it feels." The girl replies, "I don't care."	Discuss whether hurting another's feelings will solve the problem.
3. One child brings a fresh sheet of paper for the boy to use to begin a new picture.	Thank the child for this positive action and for being a good friend.

Extending the Experience

- Recognize that in mixed-age groupings, younger children often draw on older children's papers as a form of admiration. Help older children discuss this.

- Draw designs on paper. Then pass the papers around, letting everyone add details to each drawing. Display the collaborative creations for everyone to admire.

- Make a cooperative mural to go along with a theme the children are studying.

Skills Used
Social-Emotional Skills
Motor Skills
Creative Thinking Skills

Problem Solving Safari—Art

THAT'S UGLY

Your children are drawing and coloring at the art table. One child looks at a younger child's paper and says, "That's ugly." The younger child responds with tears. What can the other children do?

Children's Possible Solutions

1. A girl says, "It is *not* ugly," and an older boy says gently, "He's just a little kid." The other children look on and say nothing.

2. A girl says, "I like your picture. Let's color together and make a book."

Your Role

Facilitate discussion. Ask, "How might this child feel? How did you color when you were younger?" Help your children understand that we are all beginners sometime.

Compliment the girl on being a good friend and on recognizing how hard the younger child worked on his picture.

Extending the Experience

- View pictures of modern art with its drips and squiggles. Talk about how famous artists created the pictures.

- Visit an art museum to view modern art. Which paintings do the children like? Which do they not like? Why? Which paintings do they think that they could paint?

- Hang a gallery of artwork by children of all ages in the center's lobby or hallway where all works can be viewed and respected.

Skills Used
Social-Emotional Skills
Motor Skills

Problem Solving Safari—Art

HE'S NOT SHARING!

Your children are at the art table working on self-directed activities. One child has most of the felt tip markers and refuses to share them. "I need these," he says.

Children's Possible Solutions

1. One child begins to color with crayons. Another child uses art pastels.

2. One child suggests a rule: "If you don't share, you have to leave the art table." Another child suggests a different rule: "You can only take one marker at a time. You put it back before you take another one."

Your Role

Facilitate discussion with your children. Encourage them to look for a solution that is fair for everyone.

Discuss the suggested rules, weighing all opinions equally. Help your children come to a fair decision.

Extending the Experience

- Plan an art activity in which the children sit together in pairs and each pair shares a small basket of supplies.

- Role-play scenarios in which one or more children won't share supplies or equipment. Discuss how each person in the scenario feels.

Skills Used
Social-Emotional Skills

18 ♦ Problem Solving Safari—Art

COLORED TISSUE MARKS

Colored tissue paper was placed on a damp table. When your children remove the paper, they discover that it has left a colored mark. How did this happen?

Children's Possible Solutions

1. Your children decide to put the colored tissue in several locations, wet and dry, to see if the paper will leave a mark.

2. One child suggests trying other colors of tissue paper. Will they leave marks too?

3. Another child experiments with other kinds of paper, placing newsprint, construction paper, computer paper, and scrap paper on a dampened table.

Your Role

Encourage the children's experimenting and provide cleanup supplies at the end of the process. Ask open-ended questions such as "What will happen if you put the paper on something warm? Something rough? Does it matter if you try this inside a dark cabinet?"

Provide many colors of paper for your children to use. Ask, "Does it matter if the tissue paper is the same color as the object you put it on?"

Praise the child's experimenting and encourage her to share her results with a friend.

Extending the Experience

- Use wet, crumpled balls of tissue paper to apply color to art paper.
- Discover what can be made with colored tissue paper, glue, and paper plates.
- Make colored tissue paper collages. What happens to the colors when they overlap?

Skills Used
Critical Thinking Skills
Motor Skills

Problem Solving Safari—Art • 19

STOPPED-UP GLUE BOTTLES

The nozzles of several plastic glue bottles are stopped up. Your children squeeze and squeeze, but no glue comes out. How can the nozzles be opened?

Children's Possible Solutions

Your Role

1. One child pulls and twists and turns a nozzle cover until he pulls it off, exposing the insides. Now the glue comes out, but there is no way to control the amount or the direction.

Discuss what happened. Can anyone think of other ways to unstop the nozzles?

2. A girl suggests using scissors to pry off the dried glue around the tip of a nozzle. Another child suggests sticking something sharp down into the nozzle holes to keep them open.

Use the situation as an opportunity to discuss safety. "We use scissors just for cutting, and sharp, pointed things can hurt us." Suggest a safe alternative such as removing the glue from the nozzles with warm water.

Extending the Experience

- Together, plan an art activity that requires putting glue on paper in particular places, such as in the corners or around the edges.

- For some art projects, offer glue in small margarine tubs or film canisters and provide cotton swabs or coffee stirrers to use as applicators.

Skills Used
Critical Thinking Skills
Motor Skills

20 ♦ Problem Solving Safari—Art

DRIPPY PAINT

A child is painting at the easel. The paint is a bit thin and is dripping down the paper. What can she do?

Children's Possible Solutions

1. The child gets a facial tissue and uses it to blot up the excess paint.

2. The child uses a facial tissue like a paintbrush to smear the drippy paint across the paper.

3. Another child has been watching with interest. He thinks that the paint should be thicker.

Your Role

Acknowledge the child's resourcefulness. Make certain that lots of tissues are available.

Compliment the child on learning a new painting technique. Ask if she would like to teach it to other children.

Brainstorm with your children. What might they add to the paint to thicken it? Encourage all safe solutions and provide materials for the children to try. Offer small amounts of paint to experiment with.

Extending the Experience

- Drip small spoonfuls of paint on pieces of paper. Then tilt the papers to let the drips create colorful designs.
- Use paints of various thicknesses at the easel.
- View pictures of modern art with its drippy, splashed, and smeared techniques.

Skills Used
Critical Thinking Skills
Motor Skills

Problem Solving Safari—Art

NO PAINT-BRUSHES

Your children want to paint at the easel, but somebody forgot to put out the paintbrushes. What can the children use to make their pictures?

Children's Possible Solutions | Your Role

Children's Possible Solutions	Your Role
1. One child decides to use her fingers as a brush.	Support the child's idea. Provide soap and water for cleanup.
2. Another child suggests using cotton swabs as paintbrushes.	Acknowledge the child's creative idea and provide cotton swabs for testing.
3. A third child suggests bringing felt tip markers to the easel and using them instead of paint and brushes.	Compliment the child's problem solving idea. Discuss how drawing with markers at the easel is different from drawing with them at a table.

Extending the Experience

- Test various items from around the room to apply paint to paper.

- Use items from nature, such as twigs, leaves, or dried grass, as paintbrushes. Discuss the results.

- Hang mural paper on an outside wall. Apply paint with various kinds of old, clean brushes such as toothbrushes, scrub brushes, bottle brushes, and hairbrushes. Talk about which brushes made which designs.

Skills Used
Critical Thinking Skills
Creative Thinking Skills
Motor Skills

Problem Solving Safari—Art

WHY DOESN'T THIS STUFF STICK?

Several of your children have used paste in making their collages. As the paste dries, many of the attached materials are falling off. What can the children do about this?

Children's Possible Solutions | Your Role

1. One child applies more and more paste to his creation. Some of the collage materials seem buried in paste.	Acknowledge the child's persistence.
2. Another child applies a thick layer of glue on top of the dried paste and reattaches her collage materials.	Provide materials and encouragement.
3. A third child removes all of the collage materials remaining on his paper and places his paper and the materials in a resealable plastic bag to take home.	Compliment the child's creative approach to taking his items home.

Extending the Experience

- In separate margarine tubs, mix paste by combining flour and water. Compare and discuss the various concoctions. Which are thicker? Thinner? Which hold better?

- Compare flour and water paste with commercial paste. How are they the same? How are they different?

- Experiment with other ways to stick things together. Explore adhesive bandages, strips of prepasted wallpaper dipped in water, various tapes, rubber cement, gummed labels, and glue.

Skills Used
Critical Thinking Skills
Creative Thinking Skills
Motor Skills

Problem Solving Safari—Art

MIXING COLORS

Two of your children are painting at the easel. They discover that where the red paint and the yellow paint run together, the color becomes orange. All the children are excited. How can they make other new colors?

Children's Possible Solutions | Your Role

Children's Possible Solutions	Your Role
1. Your children decide to mix other paint colors together, two at a time.	Compliment the children on their ingenuity and supply the needed materials.
2. One child suggests mixing all the paint colors together.	Encourage the children to name the new colors they create.
3. Another child suggests mixing colors by using one color of crayon over another.	Provide crayons for experimentation.

Extending the Experience

- Use plastic dropper bottles of food coloring to experiment with color mixing at the water table.

- Mix small amounts of different-colored tempera paint on squares of white construction paper and name the colors. Gather the papers together to make a color book.

- Look through pieces cut from colored, translucent file folders. What do the children see? What do they see when they look through two or more colors at once?

Skills Used
Creative Thinking Skills
Motor Skills

24 ♦ Problem Solving Safari—Art

HOW DO YOU MAKE HANDPRINTS?

Your children have been fingerpainting. Before washing her hands, one child leans her hand on the sink, leaving a colorful handprint. The other children are fascinated and want to know how to make handprints too.

Children's Possible Solutions

Your Role

1. Your children flatten their hands onto freshly fingerpainted papers, then make handprints on the washable tabletop.

Support the children's experimentation. Provide supplies, including materials for cleanup.

2. A child at the easel paints his hands and presses them onto the easel paper, making a handprint picture.

Provide opportunities for other children to try this method.

3. Another child shows others how to make handprints by pressing her hands in wet sand.

Praise the child's creativity. Can your children think of even more ways to make handprints?

Extending the Experience

- Using a stamp pad, make fingerprints and thumbprints on paper. With fine point markers, try turning the prints into things such as bugs, tiny people, or tiny cars.

- Look for footprints left by shoes after walking through a puddle or wet grass, then onto dry pavement.

- Put a sponge in a pie plate and pour on a little paint. Press various kitchen gadgets and other items onto the sponge, then onto paper to make prints.

Skills Used
Creative Thinking Skills
Motor Skills

Problem Solving Safari—Art ◆ 25

THE MODELING DOUGH IS ICKY

The modeling dough is drying out. Its texture is uneven, and when your children use it, the dough crumbles in their hands. What can the children do?

Children's Possible Solutions

	Your Role
1. One child says that if you add water to a sponge, it gets soft. He suggests adding water to the modeling dough.	Support the activity and have your children discuss what happens.
2. Another child remembers that the dough needs to be kept in a covered container. She suggests putting a sign on the dough container: "Shut this tight."	Provide paper and felt tip markers for making the sign, and tape for attaching the sign to the container.
3. Several children remember making modeling dough in the past. They suggest making new dough.	Let each interested child make his or her own no-cook modeling dough. Then make a batch of fresh dough for the room.

Extending the Experience

- Discover and discuss different ways to work with modeling dough, such as pounding, patting, rolling, and ripping. Record the different actions on a chart.
- Use various implements, such as plastic knives, potato mashers, or garlic presses, with modeling dough.

Skills Used
Creative Thinking Skills
Motor Skills

26 ◆ Problem Solving Safari—Art

DRIED-OUT MARKERS

Your children want to use felt tip markers for an art project, but they discover that several of the markers are dried out. What can the children do?

Children's Possible Solutions

Your Role

1. One child suggests brushing water over the paper and then drawing on the wet paper with the markers.

Encourage your children to try this solution. Provide materials and discuss the results.

2. Several other children suggest soaking the markers in a tub of water.

Encourage the children to try this solution and discuss the results. If the markers do work after soaking, are the colors as bright as before? How long do the markers continue to work?

3. A girl tries coloring with crayons and brushing water over her paper to make the designs look like they were made with markers.

Encourage the child's creative solution. Discuss the results.

4. Another child says, "Someone left the tops off the markers. We shouldn't do that!"

Discuss the consequences of not replacing the marker caps at the end of art projects. Why is it important to care for materials?

Extending the Experience

- Provide new felt tip markers and celebrate their bright, vibrant colors.
- Use watercolor pencils to make designs on paper. Then paint over the designs with water to create a watercolor look.
- Paint over construction paper with buttermilk and then draw on the paper with art pastels.

Skills Used
Creative Thinking Skills
Motor Skills

Problem Solving Safari—Art

Parent Flyer
PROBLEM SOLVING WITH ART

Young children are naturally curious. Experimenting with art materials helps them find out why things happen and how things change. Manipulating and combining the materials allows children to develop their creativity and thinking skills. Provide art supplies for your child and allow freedom to explore them. Join your child in "just messing around" with art and enjoy the learning you share.

Look around you for problem solving opportunities such as those that follow. Then, with your child, have fun following the Problem Solving Steps below to arrive at possible solutions. Remember, we all learn through trial and error; there are no "perfect" answers!

Problem Solving Opportunities

Here are some problems that you and your child might encounter while doing art projects.

- You have no purple paint. How you can make some?

- Why did the modeling dough dry out? How can we prevent this from happening?

- Glue has dried on our fingers. How can we remove it?

- How can we paint a picture that looks sparkly?

Problem Solving Steps

Below are simple problem solving steps to follow. Let your child take the lead; avoid solving the problem for your child.

1. Identify and discuss the problem.

2. Brainstorm ideas for solutions.

3. Select a solution that seems workable.

4. Try out the idea.

5. Evaluate your solution. If it didn't work, try another one.

Reproducible • Totline® Publications • P.O. Box 2250, Everett, WA 98203

CHILDREN'S BOOK LIST

These books offer your children opportunities to learn about and discuss other problem solving situations related to art.

Arthur's Christmas Cookies, Lillian Hoban. Harper & Row, 1972. When Arthur makes Christmas cookies that taste terrible and are too hard to chew, he finds another use for them.

Bear's Picture, Daniel Pinkwater. E. P. Dutton, 1972. Bear meets two fine, proper gentlemen who tell him that bears can't paint pictures. Bear paints anyway—a picture that makes him happy.

The Best Present Is Me, Janet Wolf. Harper & Row, 1984. A young girl makes a birthday present for her grandmother. When the present gets lost in traveling, Grandmother helps her understand what the very best present is.

Ed Emberly's Great Thumbprint Drawing Book, Ed Emberly. Little, Brown & Company, 1977. This book shows how to add simple lines to turn thumbprints into various critters.

Eggs Mark the Spot, Mary Jane Auch. Holiday House, 1996. Pauline the hen has a special talent. Her eggs contain images of the things she sees. She uses her talent in an art museum and ultimately saves the day when her egg shows the location of an art thief. The book also contains images of famous paintings.

Harold and the Purple Crayon, Crockett Johnson. Harper Collins, 1955. Harold uses his purple crayon to draw all that he needs.

Little Blue and Little Yellow, Leo Lionni. Pantheon, 1982. A story about best friends, a little blue spot and a little yellow spot, and what happens when they hug.

The Little Painter of Sabana Grande, Patricia Maloney Markun. Illus. by Walls Casilla. Bradbury, 1992. A young boy has no art supplies. He makes paint from river clay and convinces his family to allow him to paint pictures on the outside walls of their home. Based on a true story from Panama.

Lucy's Picture, Nicola Moon. Illus. by Alex Ayliffe. Dial Books, 1995. A child in preschool creates a very special picture for her blind grandfather, one he can "see" with his hands. Her teacher is a wonderful role model for anyone wanting to support a child's artistic efforts.

No Good in Art, Miriam Cohen. Illus. Lillian Hoban. Greenwillow, 1980. A child's critical kindergarten teacher leads him to believe he is "no good in art." He no longer tries. An understanding first-grade teacher provides freedom, supports his efforts, and accepts him as an artist.

Pink Paper Swans, Virginia Kroll. Illus. by Nancy L. Clouse. William B. Eerdmans, 1994. Janetta is fascinated by the origami creations that seem to fly out of the hands of her neighbor, Mrs. Tsujimoto. In time, Janetta learns to make the creations, building a friendship and solving a financial problem at the same time.

Spot a Cat, Lucy Micklethwait. Dorling Kindersley, 1995. Children hunt for cats in pictures of great artworks from many museums.

Spot a Dog, Lucy Micklethwait. Dorling Kindersley, 1995. Children hunt for dogs in pictures of great artworks from many museums.

Teacher Resources
from Totline® Publications

Celebrations
Easy, practical ideas for celebrating holidays and special days around the world. Plus ideas for making ordinary days special.
Celebrating Likes and Differences
Small World Celebrations
Special Day Celebrations
Great Big Holiday Celebrations

Theme-A-Saurus®
Classroom-tested, around-the-curriculum activities organized into imaginative units. Great for implementing a child-directed program.
Multisensory Theme-A-Saurus
Theme-A-Saurus
Theme-A-Saurus II
Toddler Theme-A-Saurus
Alphabet Theme-A-Saurus
Nursery Rhyme Theme-A-Saurus
Storytime Theme-A-Saurus

1•2•3 Series
Open-ended, age-appropriate, cooperative, and no-lose experiences for working with preschool children.
1•2•3 Art
1•2•3 Games
1•2•3 Colors
1•2•3 Puppets
1•2•3 Reading & Writing
1•2•3 Rhymes, Stories & Songs
1•2•3 Math
1•2•3 Science
1•2•3 Shapes

Snacks Series
Easy, educational recipes for healthy eating and expanded learning.
Super Snacks
Healthy Snacks
Teaching Snacks
Multicultural Snacks

Piggyback® Songs
New songs sung to the tunes of childhood favorites. No music to read! Easy for adults and children to learn. Chorded for guitar or autoharp.
Piggyback Songs
More Piggyback Songs
Piggyback Songs for Infants & Toddlers
Piggyback Songs in Praise of God
Piggyback Songs in Praise of Jesus
Holiday Piggyback Songs
Animal Piggyback Songs
Piggyback Songs for School
Piggyback Songs to Sign
Spanish Piggyback Songs
More Piggyback Songs for School

Busy Bees
These seasonal books help two- and three-year-olds discover the world around them through their senses. Each book includes fun activity and learning ideas, songs, snack ideas, and more!
Busy Bees—SPRING
Busy Bees—SUMMER
Busy Bees—FALL
Busy Bees—WINTER

101 Tips for Directors
Great ideas for managing a preschool or daycare. These hassle-free, handy hints are a great help.
Staff and Parent Self-Esteem
Parent Communication
Health and Safety
Marketing Your Center
Resources for You and Your Center
Child Development Training

101 Tips for Toddler Teachers
Designed for adults who work with toddlers.
Classroom Management
Discovery Play
Dramatic Play
Large Motor Play
Small Motor Play
Word Play

101 Tips for Preschool Teachers
Valuable, fresh ideas for adults who work with young children.
Creating Theme Environments
Encouraging Creativity
Developing Motor Skills
Developing Language Skills
Teaching Basic Concepts
Spicing Up Learning Centers

Problem Solving Safari
This unique series teaches teachers to help children problem-solve and think for themselves. Each book includes scenarios from children's real play and possible solutions.
Problem Solving Safari—Art
Problem Solving Safari—Blocks
Problem Solving Safari— Dramatic Play
Problem Solving Safari— Manipulatives
Problem Solving Safari— Outdoors
Problem Solving Safari— Science

The Best of Totline® Series
Collections of some of the finest, most useful material published in *Totline Magazine* over the years.
The Best of Totline
The Best of Totline Parent Flyers

Early Learning at its Best

For parents and children: books, posters, puzzles and more from Totline® Publications

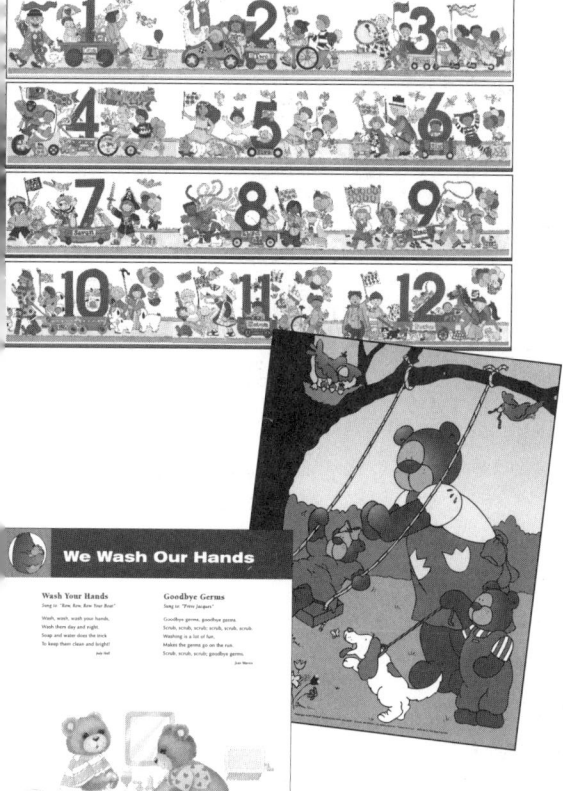

A Year of Fun
Age-specific books detailing how young children grow and change and what parents can do to lay a strong foundation for later learning.
- **Just for Babies**
- **Just for Ones**
- **Just for Twos**
- **Just for Threes**
- **Just for Fours**
- **Just for Fives**

Getting Ready for School
Fun, easy-to-follow ideas for developing essential skills that preschoolers need before they can successfully achieve higher levels of learning.
- **Ready to Learn Colors, Shapes, and Numbers**
- **Ready to Write and Develop Motor Skills**
- **Ready to Read**
- **Ready to Communicate**
- **Ready to Listen and Explore the Senses**

Learning Everywhere
Teaches parents to become aware of the everyday opportunities for teaching their children about language, art, science, math, problem solving, self-esteem, and more!
- **Teaching House**
- **Teaching Town**
- **Teaching Trips**

Beginning Fun With Art
Introduce young children to the fun of art while developing coordination skills and building self-confidence.
- **Craft Sticks • Crayons • Felt**
- **Glue • Paint • Paper Shapes**
- **Modeling Dough • Yarn**
- **Tissue Paper • Scissors**
- **Rubber Stamps • Stickers**

Beginning Fun With Science
Make science fun with these quick, safe, easy-to-do activities that lead to discovery and spark the imagination.
- **Bugs & Butterflies**
- **Plants & Flowers**
- **Magnets**
- **Rainbows & Colors**
- **Sand & Shells**
- **Water & Bubbles**

Teaching Tales
Each of these children's books includes a delightful story plus related activity ideas that expand on the story's theme.
- **Kids Celebrate the Alphabet**
- **Kids Celebrate Numbers**
- **Ellie the Evergreen**
- **The Wishing Fish**
- **The Bear and the Mountain**
- **Huff and Puff's Snowy Day**
- **Huff and Puff on Groundhog Day**
- **Huff and Puff's Hawaiian Rainbow**
- **Huff and Puff Go to Camp**
- **Huff and Puff on Fourth of July**
- **Huff and Puff Around the World**
- **Huff and Puff Go to School**
- **Huff and Puff on Halloween**
- **Huff and Puff on Thanksgiving**
- **Huff and Puff's Foggy Christmas**

Learning Puzzles
Designed to challenge as children grow. Each giant floor puzzle offers learning opportunities, plus teaches basic matching and thinking skills.
- **Kids Celebrate Numbers Beginning Floor Puzzle**
- **Kids Celebrate the Alphabet Beginning Floor Puzzle**
- **Bear Hugs 4-in-1 Puzzle Set**
- **Busy Bees 4-in-1 Puzzle Set**

Two-Sided Circle Puzzles
Double-sided, giant floor puzzles designed in a circle with cutout pieces for extra learning and fun.
- **Underwater Adventure**
- **African Adventure**

Work and Play Together Posters
A colorful collection of cuddly bear posters showing adult and children bears playing and working together. Each 17"x 22".
- **We Build Together**
- **We Cook Together**
- **We Play Together**
- **We Read Together**
- **We Sing Together**
- **We Work Together**

Bear Hugs® Sing-Along Health Posters
Encourage young children to develop good health habits with these posters. Additional learning activities on back!
- **We Brush Our Teeth**
- **We Can Exercise**
- **We Cover our Coughs and Sneezes**
- **We Eat Good Food**
- **We Get Our Rest**
- **We Wash Our Hands**

Totline products are available at fine parent and teacher stores.

For the dealer nearest you, call 1-800-421-5565.

If you like Totline® Books, You'll love Totline® Magazine!

Bonus Poster Inside!

Totline MAGAZINE
Active preschool learning at its best

Flying High with Windy Day Fun

Focus on **Eyes** Activities Worth a Look

Discovering **Purple**

SHE'S COLORING ON MY PAPER
Problem-Solving Tips

Looking At **Yellow**
How many yellow things can you find?

For fresh ideas that challenge and engage young children in active learning, reach for **Totline® Magazine**—Proven ideas from innovative teachers!

FREE full-color poster in each issue!

Each issue includes
- Seasonal learning themes
- Stories, songs, and rhymes
- Open-ended art projects
- Science explorations
- Reproducible parent pages
- Ready-made teaching materials
- Activities just for toddlers
- Reproducible healthy snack recipes

Receive a FREE copy of Totline® Magazine by calling 800-609-1724 for subscription information.